THE RULE OF LAW

VOLUME 1, ISSUE 4 OF BRILLOPEDIA

K. SANJANA

ISBN 979-888503996-3

Contents

Preface

"Start writing, no matter what. The water does not flow until the faucet is turned on".

-Louis L'Amour

Hundreds of students and professors are contributing their work to Brillopedia, we are here to provide ample information about Law and Contemporary issues. Our aim is to provide a platform for today's generation to express their views and ideas on law and contemporary law.

Publication

This research paper is published in volume 1, issue 4 of Brillopedia

Author

K. Sanjana

CHAPTER ONE

ABSTRACT

The concept of Rule of Law is that the state is governed, not by the ruler or the nominated representatives of the people but by the law. The Constitution of India intended for India to be a country governed by the rule of law. It provides that the constitution shall be the supreme power in the land and the legislative and the executive derive their authority from the constitution. The King is not the law but the law is king. It means that the law rules over all people including the persons administering the law. The law makers need to give reasons that can be justified under the law while exercising their powers to make and administer law. Rule of Law plays an important role in the democratic countries. It provides protection to the people against the arbitrary action of the administrative authorities. The expression 'rule of law' has been derived from the French phrase 'la Principle de legality' i.e. a government based on the principles of law. In simple words, the term 'rule of law, indicates the state of affairs in a country where, in main, the law rules. Law may be taken to mean mainly a rule or principle which governs the external actions of the human beings and which is recognized and applied by the State in the administration of justice. It is impossible to get the supremacy of law without the rule of law

The concept of the rule of law is specified by the roles that a legal system plays. Theorists of the rule of law have produced lists of these roles, these lists can be subsequently categorized in terms of focus on form, substance, and procedure.19 understanding these three aspects helps us in focusing our search for the broad concept of the rule of law. lon fuller advocates that people need to live within a framework of predictability. Therefore, the form of a lawmaking is crucial determining its legitimacy. For example, imagine a system in which laws are only created ex post facto and apply to actions after the fact. Certainly, it is illegitimate to punish individuals for actions that have occurred in the past before a law was in place. Alternatively, imagine a case in which the lawmaker changes the law each day. it is similarly ludicrous that individuals be held liable for laws that change every day, or hour, or even minute. These two formal characteristics of legal systems, prospectivity and stability, are two of eight characteristics laid forth by lon fuller. the full list includes: 1. generality, for laws must exist in general, rather than on an ad hoc basis; 2. publicity, for laws must be publicized, particularly to those parties affected; 3. prospectivity, for lawmakers must not abuse retroactive legislation; 4. intelligibility, for laws must be understandable; 5. consistency, for laws must not be contradictory; 6. practicability, for laws must require conduct within the scope of the powers of the affected party; 7. stability, for laws must be consistent in order to be followed; and 8. congruence, for laws must be administered in the way that they are announced. Fuller argues that laws must fulfil all of these formal characteristics to be legitimate. He, like waldron, claims that understanding the concept of the rule of law is crucial in bestowing legitimacy of a legal system; however, he places particular emphasis on these formal characteristics. Fuller claims that "a total failure in any one of these eight directions does not simply result in a bad system of law; it results in something that is not properly called a legal system at all. These criteria are not simply suggestions, but requirements for a legal system's legitimacy in the eyes of its subjects.

CHAPTER TWO

DICEY CONCEPT

Dicey is one of the well-known jurists of England and he has written a famous book "law of the constitution". One should know the difference between administrative law and the rule of law. People who are in government job have different law from ordinary citizens and the rule of law is equal for everyone whether he is prime minister of India or a normal clerk working in an office. The same law will be applicable to both of them, no discrimination will be done under the rule of law and rule of law is supreme in nature.

Dicey was against making different rules for a different class of people so he stood by against this concept and promoted the idea of rule of law. Here a term is used **"droit administrative"**was introduced by napoleon and in france, it was known as droitadministratiff. France was having separate administrative court for dealing with the matter. According to this action by the citizens against an official for a wrongful act committed in their official capacity will be dealt by the special court not by the ordinary courts of law. droitadministratiff does not consist of rules and law made by the french parliament but it includes a rule which is developed by the judges of the administrative court.

CHAPTER THREE

THE DOCTRINE OF RULE OF LAW HAS 3 MEANING IN DICEY BOOK

1. Supremacy of law.
2. Equality before the law.
3. The predominance of a legal spirit.

Merit and demerits of the dicey concept

MERITS

1. Help in making limits to the power of administrative authorities.
2. A major role in growth and recognition of administrative law.
3. Act as a scale for the test of administrative action.

DEMERITS

1. His theory was not fully accepted during that era also.
2. Failed to distinguish between discretionary and arbitrary power.
3. He misunderstood the concept of droit administration which was actually successful in France.

RULE OF LAW

Rule of law is a product of struggle by the people from centuries for recognition of their inherent rights and the concept of a rule is very ancient and old. During the ancient times, the concept of rule of law was discussed by the Greek philosopher Aristotle and Plato at the time of 350 BC so now you can imagine how old this concept. Plato has written that if rule of law under the supervision of any law than it doesn't have any value and the concept of state will get collapsed and if the law is master of government and government work as a slave for law then the concept of state will work effectively and humans can enjoy their rights.

This phrase was derived from the French phrase *"la Principe de legality"*which means that the principle of legality whatever the legal system principle is called a rule of law. Which refers to government is based on the principles not on any individuals and according to the law everything will move. Rule of law is the basic principle of the English constitution and this doctrine is accepted by the us and as well as India also.

The entire basis of administrative law is the rule of law and delegated legislation is the backbone of administrative law.

CHAPTER FOUR

DEVELOPMENT

Rule of law was developed by a British jurist albert Venn dicey in his book called "the law of the constitution" 1885. In this book, he develops this concept and he identifies 3 principles while establishing the rule of law.

According to albert Venn dicey rule of law first meaning is *"no man is punishable except for a distinct breach of law"* established in the ordinary legal manner before the ordinary court. the government or any high-class authority cannot punish any individual on the personal ground till the time an individual has committed an offence and if the offence is committed then proper procedure and trail will be conducted and in case the final verdict is that the offence is committed then physical or economic punishment will be given to the accused person. This clearly indicates that even if 100 criminals are not arrested is ok rather than punishing one innocent person.

The basic elements of that jurisprudence can be summarized as follows. The first dimension, authorization, is the very basic demand that government action have a valid legal source. a starting premise of this administrative jurisprudence is that authorization is personal to the officeholder, rather than an impersonal vesting of power in the government as a whole. the idea is that each officer vested with legal authority has responsibility to reach an independent judgment about what the statute requires, a judgment not to be supplanted by that of superiors. This responsibility precludes the spectre of a bureaucracy dictated by role-based compliance up the chain of command in which only the highest-level official bears genuine accountability. In other words, when role is defined in terms of independent judgment, role-based compliance privileges an official's independent evaluation over political loyalty or bureaucratic order. If individual judgment by agency officials is a structural premise for the rule of law within the administrative state, then it makes sense that the other aspects of the rule of law will apply to how agency officials exercise their discretion. That holds with regard to the principles of notice, justification, and coherence.

the second dimension, the cluster of values relating to notice—principles of publicity, clarity, prospectivity, and stability prominent in professor lon fuller's account of law's virtues12 12 see lon l. fuller, the morality of law 46–90 (rev. ed. 1969) (arguing these values are fundamental to law)....—has been thought to pose particular problems for the regulatory state. Regulatory statutes—the statutes that create and delegate to agencies authority to make law—are famously broad and vague. but because notice values seek to protect law's capacity to guide action, they should apply to the sources of law that directly bind private parties. in our government, that means a critical battleground for these principles is the law issued by agencies because that regulatory law, rather than the legislation authorizing the agencies to act, bears the weight of imposing obligations on private persons. once these notice values are seen as applicable to the law agencies issue, there are grounds to ask how well agencies are meeting these demands. in this vein, if rules generally fare better with regard to notice values than adjudication, then there are reasons to require agencies to, at a minimum, justify opting for adjudication instead of rulemaking. This focus also suggests agencies have an obligation, when rulemaking is not practicable, to issue some kind of guidance document reflecting the agency's best view of the statute's requirements.

Focusing on the rule of law's requirements of administrative institutions, some principles can be left to the side and some have greater importance those elements that pertain to criminal sanctions and processes have less relevance, at least if we focus on those aspects of administrative governance that are not involved in criminal justice. Likewise, other general virtues, such as compliance with the law, do not distinctively apply to administrative institutions. The conditions under which administrative bodies operate make other elements of the rule of law more central. The fact that agencies only have authority that has been delegated to them suggests the critical importance of the principle that official action be authorized. the fact that many statutes that delegate regulatory authority grant broad discretion to officials suggests the importance of notice, coherence, and justification.this insistence on decisional allocation thus can be seen as grounded in a pragmatic principle that there is a greater chance of decision in accordance with the law when officials view their duties and powers as personal, requiring their independent judgment, and not subject to supplanting by others. This idea can be put in terms of the definition of role for administrative actors. When the legal role of those delegated statutory power is defined as requiring their independent judgment, the specter of role-based compliance up a chain of command is diminished. Institutionally, this role specification spreads accountability through the bureaucracy. All those with legally delegated authority must exercise their own independent legal judgment; as a result, administrative action will represent the views of many actors, and accountability cannot be confined to the officials at the peak of the institutional hierarchy. These ideas about the foundation for decisional allocation might be formulated in terms of the following rule-of-law principle for administration: legal authorization (and duty) is relative to officeholders, not an impersonal authorization to government as a whole.

While this principle is articulated at a relatively high level of generality, it takes a stance on the contested question of the president's powers over law administration. Understanding this legal allocation—that the discretion and duty is personal to the official—clarifies how an official delegated with statutory power is to understand prodding from a president or his immediate advisors. The official is not to take that direction "as a command that she has a legal as well as a political obligation to honor, and for whose justifications she thus has no particular responsibility."

If agency officials are creating law under broad standards, they have obligations to do so in ways that provide adequate notice and justification and also respond to the values of coherence. Finally, to the extent that agencies are engaged in adjudication, the values of procedural fairness apply. This suggests focus on the following five elements or dimensions of the rule of law.

1. Authorization is a bedrock principle of liberalism and the rule of law; it ensures that the state only act or constrict an individual's liberty when authorized to do so.
2. Notice. many of the most commonly identified features of the rule of law pertain to a cluster of characteristics that help to ensure that law has the capacity to be practical in the sense of providing guidance to an individual's actions and allowing individuals to plan with some knowledge of the law. the principles of publicity, clarity, consistency, prospectivity, and stability are among the most important of these values.

3. Justification an important strain of thought about the rule of law focuses on the role of justification and argumentation in law. Justification provides protection against arbitrariness; part of what defines arbitrary action is action that is not justified.

4. Coherencelaw presents itself as a system in which norms fit together it is from the perspective of the private party—the individual or firm subject to law's demands—that coherence matters. "For citizens, law is inevitably an integral system, premised in contemporary social expectations and political judgments; a person interested in her legal obligations looks to the whole environment, not a disordered collection of fragmentary, isolated, mutually independent pieces."

5. Proceduralfairness. A central virtue of the rule of law is procedural fairness, that is, the set of institutional arrangements that provide an unbiased determination of one's rights and duties through transparent procedures with determinations based on evidence. Here the rule of law joins company with the most basic elements of due process, though it can be more demanding.

Summaryevaluating administrative law through the lens of these five dimensions of the rule of law exposes some long-established practices as having troublesome rule-of-law foundations and reveals that other contested practices are well grounded in rule-of-law values. the closest match between the rule-of-law principles and current doctrine and practice is justification; administrative law and practice represents as well as any domain of law the sense in which law is ultimately argumentative.

the idea that agencies have duties to assist in integrating statutory law into the larger fabric of law, and thus to be partners with courts in implementing the law in a coherent fashion, while not as well-established as the agency's duties of reasoned elaboration, is steadily gaining recognition. This analysis highlights the rule-of-law foundation for that duty.

With respect to notice principles, more groundbreaking work is required. Some of it will take the form of holding agencies to the basic principles of notice, as current scholarship has done with regard to the fundamental value of publicity in agency rules. Further work could also form an executive or judicial requirement for agencies to justify their decision when they opt not to proceed through rulemaking, a departure from long-settled law. it could also usefully involve embracing or even imposing a duty upon agencies to issue, in the form of guidance, their best general statement of the law's requirements when rulemaking is not practicable.

Perhaps the most controversial analysis pertains to the principle of authorization. Both principles—decisional allocation within the executive branch and courts giving weight to agencies' views of the scope of their own authority—have waxed and waned in terms of their embrace in the law. Today these positions, at least based on intimations from the Supreme Court, may be on the wane. If so, there is all the more reason to highlight the ways in which officials conceive of their statutory obligations as personal anchors and reinforces the government's commitment to the law. And once so conceived the grounds for recognizing that independent review—whether for agency officials or courts—does not require eschewing respectful consideration of the positions of other government officials become all the stronger.

9 798888 503996